Truth and Treason

Rahul Varma

We acknowledge the support of the Canada Council for the Arts for our publishing program. We also acknowledge support from the Government of Ontario through the Ontario Arts Council.

ONTARIO ARTS COUNCIL
CONSEIL DES ARTS DE L'ONTARIO
an Ontario government agency
un organisme du gouvernement de l'Ontario

Canada Council   Conseil des arts
for the Arts   du Canada

For professional or amateur production rights, please contact:

Michael Petrasek
Kensington Literary Representation
34 St. Andrew Street, Toronto, ON, Canada, M5T 1K6
416.848.9648   kensingtonlit@rogers.com

Cover photo, and photos on pp 12, 28, 35, 58, and 63, by Terry Hughes. Reproduced with permission.

Cover design by Rajinder Arora.

Truth and Treason has been translated into Hindi/Urdu by Uma Jhunjhunwala as *Dhokha*, and produced multiple times by The Little Thespian Company in India under the direction of Dr. S.M. Azhar Alam

Library and Archives Canada Cataloguing in Publication

Varma, Rahul, author

    Truth and reason / Rahul Varma.

Issued in print and electronic formats.

ISBN 978-1-988449-06-7 (softcover).--ISBN 978-1-988449-07-4 (HTML)

    I. Title.

PS8593.A74T78 2017   C812'.54   C2017-901855-8

                                       C2017-901856-6

Printed and bound in Canada by Coach House Printing.

Mawenzi House Publishers Ltd.
39 Woburn Avenue (B)
Toronto, Ontario M5M 1K5
Canada
www.mawenzihouse.com

Truth and Treason

Acknowledgement

I wish to acknowledge the support of the Canada Council for the Arts, which awarded me a grant to write *Truth and Treason*; Factory Theatre, Toronto, which generously supported the development of *Truth and Treason* through the Crosscurrents play development program; Shastri Indo-Canadian Institute for awarding me the art fellowship to work under the guidance of the late Habib Tanvir in India; Soheil Parsa and Guillermo Verdecchia for their brilliant dramaturgy; Arianna Bardesono for her confidence in my work; Dipti Gupta, my wife, for her critical feedback; Aliya Varma, our daughter, who rewrote many lines of the play and refined the writing with me; my mother Krishna Varma, who taught me resilience and commitment by example; Dr. Daya Varma, my father, for his keen political observations; Dr. Denis Salter and Ken McDonough for their wisdom and feedback; Edward (Ted) Little, ex-editor of theatre quarterly *alt. theatre*—I named the captain Edward to honour Ted's virtues and commitment to theatre; Linda Levesque and Stephanie Lambert, whatever was needed they found a way to do it; and finally my family, in Canada and in India—their presence is a comfort.

Rahul Varma

This one is for Aliya

and

in memory of

Dr. Habib Tanvir (1923–2009),
whose invaluable guidance cannot be expressed in one line.

Preface

During the production of my play *Zahreeli Hawa,* the Hindi translation of *Bhopal,* I asked my long-time friend and mentor, iconic Indian playwright and director Habib Tanvir, a question: What justification could there be for the US to invade an entire country to punish a handful of suspected terrorists while the culprit of the Bhopal disaster—the CEO of Union Carbide, twenty-five thousand deaths on his resumé—roamed free in the US? Habib Tanvir, in turn, answered by asking if I wanted to write a play on the subject. I said yes and sought his guidance. He told me that I must pose new and difficult questions long suppressed by governments and media. He told me to identify the unidentified terrorists and to examine the nature of their actions.

Tanvir explained that we must distinguish a legitimate struggle for liberation from terrorism that is an act of desperation. He said that although terrorism is incapable of solving the very desperation that gives rise to it, we must understand who the terrorists are and why they resort to terror for political goals. What are their goals and how do they manage to capture the attention of Western governments? In contrast, who are the legitimate freedom fighters and why is their cause ignored and misunderstood? Whose purpose is served by this misunderstanding? Can terrorism be defeated by invading a country alleged to be harbouring terrorists? How can a democratic state justify invading another country in the name of the common good? Who decides where and when democracy is lacking? What kind of democracy can be imposed by aggression rather than by popular decision? What must be the consequences of collusion in lies about destroying weapons of mass destruction, or improving the status of women? My conversation with Tanvir resulted in my second collaboration with him—*Truth and Treason.*

Like Bhopal and *Zahreeli Hawa,* the writing of Truth and Treason started with him, but our face-to-face interaction was limited by the fact that he stayed in India and I in Canada. I received his feedback via emails and phone conversations, which at times sounded incomplete due to the distance. But what gave me confidence was the fact that he had given his blessing to the project.

Tanvir supported the idea that the play must not be documentary theatre comprised of only facts. Unlike many war-related plays that are written these days—most based on documentary evidence and testimonies—Tanvir guided me to write a play that would go beyond documentary realities. He told me that a play is not about representing realities but about finding truth, and an imagined story is the best forum capable of doing that. And he supported the idea that the play must have Iraqi characters to play Iraqi roles and that their roles must be substantial.

The play was written and workshopped at the Crosscurrents play development program at Factory Theatre in Toronto. It was publicly read twice at Factory in 2006 and 2007. I then received the support of the Shastri Indo-Canadian Institute, which gave me the opportunity to spend two months in India working with Tanvir. The script was refined and rewritten under his dispassionate and critical dramaturgical supervision. Once a new draft was created, actor David Francis, a frequent visitor of India, read the text to Tanvir, who was impressed enough that he expressed a desire to come to Canada to direct the play, despite his ill health. That could not happen. Habib Tanvir passed away on June 8, 2009.

The 9/11 terrorist attack on the World Trade Centre was an unconscionable act, but so was the US invasion in the name of destroying weapons of mass destruction, bringing about a change in regime, and installing democracy. What kind of democracy would it be if installed by an invasion rather than by popular decision? What are we to make of a war waged in the name of destroying weapons of mass destruction which have never been found? What about the lives wasted and a country destroyed?

George Bush justified war by manufacturing lies. He took war politics to its lowest depths. He manufactured lies about weapons of mass destruction (WMDs) and used Colin Powell, the vulnerable black secretary of state, to make a case for the invasion, knowing full well that the WMDs did not exist. He mandated Powell to establish links between Al-Qaeda and the weapons of mass destruction. Powell embarrassed himself and consequently resigned his post. But Bush went on to say that it would be "suicidal" for the US not to attack Iraq. And we once again witnessed the most powerful country in the world declaring war against a sovereign nation based on manufactured paranoia; a nation that had been, until yesterday, a friend. Iraq is the latest addition to the list of friends turned into foes, a list that includes Cuba, Nicaragua, Libya, Grenada, and Panama. The new policy arising from the paranoia was a pre-emptive strike. Bush simply declared that Saddam Hussein was a homicidal dictator and that Iraq needed a regime change. In other words, the United States could do whatever the hell it wanted to.

The most recent war in Iraq was not a war against terrorism, it *was* terrorism. We must look for ways to end the terrorism of war.

Rahul Varma

February 2015

Characters

Captain Edward Alston: The officer in charge of the checkpoint Backwoods, behind which the Conference for Democracy and the Salvation of Iraq is taking place.

Commander Hektor Frank: A top-ranking military officer who also acts as a liaison between the military in Iraq and the political leadership in Washington.

Kendra Cox: A black woman who is the finance officer responsible for the reconstruction of Iraq. She is the organizer of the Conference for Democracy and the Salvation of Iraq.

Omar Abdul Ahad: A secular writer, playwright, and poet.

Nahla Abdul Ahad: A Canadian woman of Arab descent who is married to Omar Ahad.

Samir Raghib: An Iraqi Canadian who has a special UN pass to enter all checkpoints.

Ahmed Aziz: An Iraqi policeman and interpreter who assists Edward.

Prime Minister: The exiled leader who is appointed as the prime minister of Iraq by the Americans.

Sheik: A clergyman who has an uneasy and complex relationship with Omar Ahad.

Chorus: playing street people, medical crew, watchtower, headquarters, etc.

The clergyman and the prime minister can be played by the same actor.

Production

Truth and Treason was first produced by Teesri Duniya Theatre at the Monument-National in Montreal from September 8 to 19, 2009, with the following cast and creative team:

Nahla Abdul Ahad:	Christine Aubin Khalifah
Omar Abdul Ahad: z	Abdelghafour Elaaziz
Ghazal Abdul Ahad:	Charley Husknost
Commander Hektor Frank:	David Francis
Captain Edward Alston:	Alex Ivanovici
Ahmed Aziz:	Karim Babin
Kendra Cox:	Warona Setshwaelo
Samir Raghib:	Jean-Moïse Martin
Trista Sanchar:	Sarah Garton Stanley
Prime Minister & Sheik:	Ivan Smith

The watchtower voice, headquarters voice, and two soldiers were played by Alex Ivanovici and Karim Babin

Director:	Arianna Bardesono
Assistant Director:	Maya Dhawan
Stage Manager:	Kathryn Cleveland
Assistant Stage Manager:	Michael Panich
Accent Consultant:	Rea Nolan

Set Design:	Romain Fabre
Sound Design:	Jesse Ash
Lighting Design:	Kirsten Watt
Costume Design:	Ève-line Leduc
Hair and Makeup Design:	Natasha Rosdol
Musician and Player:	Abdelghafour Elaaziz
Poster Design:	Tracy Martin
Production Manager:	Dave Surette
Production, Media, and Public Relations:	Stephanie Lambert
Production Assistant:	Michelle Smushkevitch
General Manager:	Linda Levesque

Note: After the premiere production, the character of journalist Trista Sanchar was dropped. Ghazal's character is implied but not physically present in this draft. The soldiers have also been removed.

Scene 1

Iraq under the American occupation, late 2007.

GHAZAL runs on in fear. An exchange between military personnel is heard offstage.

GHAZAL	Baba, come home... come home, Baba...
WATCHTOWER	Patrol to headquarters.
HEADQUARTERS	Headquarters. Go ahead.
WATCHTOWER	We've spotted an Iraqi female running towards the checkpoint.
HEADQUARTERS	Where is she now?
WATCHTOWER	Five hundred metres from the checkpoint...
HEADQUARTERS	Identify the female...
WATCHTOWER	Small, under four feet, three hundred metres from the checkpoint.
HEADQUARTERS	Stop her.
WATCHTOWER	Two hundred metres... now.
HEADQUARTERS	Stop her...
WATCHTOWER	One hundred metres...

A gunshot.

GHAZAL	Baba...
WATCHTOWER	Looks like one of the positions just dropped her.
HEADQUARTERS	Move in and confirm.

Men and women have begun to gather around the fallen girl. SAMIR steps out from the crowd and picks up the girl's body. AHMED steps forward.

AHMED	Hey, you... mister... Put that body down.

SAMIR puts GHAZAL down.

SAMIR	She's alive.

AHMED	Move back!

SAMIR reaches for his ID.

SAMIR	Samir Raghib, UN Field Officer.

AHMED shows his badge to SAMIR.

AHMED	Ahmed Aziz, joint US–Iraqi battalion, Contact Officer, assistant to Captain Edward Alston, checkpoint Backwoods.
SAMIR	Good, then let's help this child.

AHMED snatches away SAMIR's ID card.

AHMED	You from Canada?
SAMIR	Check my ID, front and back.
AHMED	What's on the back?
SAMIR	Same thing but in French!
AHMED	Why in French?
SAMIR	I'm from Canada.
AHMED	Canada is in France?
SAMIR	Look, Mr. Contact Officer, I've a right to enter restricted zones at any time!
AHMED	Okay!
SAMIR	I know this girl's father, I know her mother, and I know where she lives.
AHMED	Then tell her mother we have taken her to the army clinic behind the checkpoint.

AHMED lifts the girl's body. The sound of an ambulance fades into the sound of an incoming helicopter.

Scene 2

KENDRA steps off the helicopter. HEKTOR welcomes her. A second helicopter has brought Iraqi exiles and opposition parties to the Conference for Democracy and the Salvation of Iraq.

HEKTOR   Ms. Cox. Kendra, welcome back to Iraq.

KENDRA   Good to be here, Commander. Is that the Iraqi contingent?

HEKTOR   All three hundred of them. There, that is Jalal Talabani. He wants to kill Masoud Barzani, if Barzani doesn't get Talabani first. But no one has been killed yet. They are happy to be coming home.

KENDRA   Commander, who do they represent?

HEKTOR   Barzani represents the northwest and Talabani the southwest.

KENDRA   And that turbaned guy?

HEKTOR   Abdul Aziz al-Hakim.

KENDRA   Who does he represent?

HEKTOR   Islamists and jihadists who hate Assyrian and Chaldean Christians, who, mind you, hate each other more than they hate Muslims...

KENDRA   And that one... the one in the suit and silk tie... the smooth-faced man.

HEKTOR   Ahmed Chalabi.

KENDRA   Who does he hate?

HEKTOR   Everybody! He's sort of a secular type who starts meetings by reciting the Koran, but was convicted of fraud *in absentia*.

KENDRA   How will we be able to handle these men at a conference meant to rebuild Iraq?

HEKTOR   That is why we waited until after Ramadan to hold your conference. Ramadan makes them crankier. They fast from sun-up to sundown and then eat all night long. Then they go to the mosque in the morning to feast on sermons from ranting imams low on protein 'n' high on passion. Finally the head imam declares the end of Ramadan by firing cannons... Boom.

EDWARD enters with AHMED.

On the other hand, there are pluses to Ramadan...

KENDRA	I'd like to hear them.
HEKTOR	They don't lie, don't steal, and don't set off bombs... Hello, Ed.
EDWARD	Commander!
HEKTOR	I think you guys know each other. Kendra Cox, the chargé d'affaires for the Conference for Democracy and the Salvation of Iraq. Captain Alston is in charge of the conference checkpoint.

HEKTOR notices AHMED.

EDWARD	My assistant and translator, Police Sergeant Ahmed Aziz, jack of all trades!
AHMED	I help Captain Edward deal with local troubles. Like this injured girl, sir.

HEKTOR studies AHMED as if he is contemplating something.

EDWARD	We've had an incident. The watchtower dropped a local earlier. She was running towards the checkpoint. Wouldn't stop, apparently! But it turns out she's just a kid. A ten-year-old girl! Wasn't carrying anything...
KENDRA	Anything I need to worry about?
EDWARD	Nothing that we can't handle! Commander gave me an extra two hundred FIF.
HEKTOR	Free Iraq Force! These privates can handle anything.
AHMED	They better not try their funny stuff with the females

here—the mullahs will cut off their privates, sir... in public. I promise!

KENDRA	*(chuckling)* Oh well, I promised Washington Iraq will be rebuilt by commerce, not by combat.
HEKTOR	Not until we win the war on terror. We are doing God's work. The people of the Babylonian desert have got to see our president's good deeds. Who in the world would dish out trillions to reconstruct a broken nation?
EDWARD	Conference security protocol is well in place.
HEKTOR	Now, make sure Ms. Cox is shown to her quarters.
EDWARD	With pleasure...
HEKTOR	Captain, Ms. Cox, this conference is in your hands.
	(to AHMED) I'd like to see you for a moment. I've a task for you.
EDWARD	Ahmed, go with Commander Frank.

HEKTOR leaves and AHMED follows.

KENDRA	Captain Alston... did you ever think we'd meet here in the ruins of Iraq?
EDWARD	Seems you'll come to any ruins I go to.
KENDRA	I can't believe I left Washington where I shook hands with heads of state and dined with the president to come to this shattered country to host a conference of returning exiles...
EDWARD	Let me take you to your quarters before the hide 'n' seek starts.
KENDRA	What is that?
EDWARD	Locals attack the checkpoint and we push them back. They return, and we push them back again. It's been a routine, except today they might stick around because a ten-year-old girl was shot and everyone is angry!
KENDRA	I hope no one blows up the conference.

EDWARD	You are one hundred percent focused on the conference.
KENDRA	No, I'm one hundred percent focused on you.

EDWARD looks at her, surprised at her confession.

A successful conference means a speedy end to the war—and that means you and I go home sooner.

EDWARD	Let me take you to the Hamra complex before the terrorists prove you wrong.

EDWARD starts to leave with KENDRA. A bomb explodes.

Just when I didn't want it to start...

Scene 3

Later, at the checkpoint, EDWARD and AHMED await NAHLA, who enters, worried, accompanied by SAMIR.

NAHLA My daughter... please, they took my daughter.

EDWARD Who?

NAHLA Soldiers! They shot my little girl.

EDWARD Calm down, ma'am.

SAMIR She needs to see her little girl.

NAHLA He saw them taking her.

EDWARD Calm down, ma'am.

SAMIR Her child is injured and you say calm down?

EDWARD You calm down, okay?

NAHLA Her name is Ghazal; she's ten.

AHMED Was she among the children who burnt a bus yesterday?

NAHLA No!

EDWARD Why was she running to the checkpoint?

NAHLA To find her father...

EDWARD Where?

AHMED *(panicked)* Captain, insurgents are closing in...

EDWARD Don't panic.

AHMED Don't panic? Do you see those angry bearded men?

AHMED points towards the signs.

Do you not see the Allah is Great signs that have gone up? There is a mini uprising.

EDWARD turns to NAHLA.

EDWARD Let me see what I can do for the lady.

NAHLA Please, yes.

EDWARD	Fill this out.
SAMIR	There is no time for protocol, Captain!
NAHLA	I'll fill in whatever form you want me to... give it to me...

She snatches the form from EDWARD and starts to fill it in. EDWARD grabs the satellite phone and dials.

EDWARD	Captain Ed Alston, 760643, Checkpoint Backwoods, come in... Yes, okay, Captain Ed Alston here... Was there an injured subject brought in today?
SAMIR	I saw it with my own eyes.

AHMED grabs SAMIR's arm and drags him away.

AHMED	You keep your mouth shut, mister.
SAMIR	I'm doing my job.

AHMED points at SAMIR's UN ID.

AHMED	When did working for the UN become a job?
SAMIR	When did holding children behind a checkpoint become a job?

AHMED grabs SAMIR with a sudden burst of anger, pulling out a knife and pushing it against SAMIR's throat.

AHMED	One more word like that from your mouth and I'll cut out your tongue and watch you bleed. Do you know how many children were orphaned? Do you know how many fathers and mothers were slaughtered? Do you know who butchered them? Where are they now? I don't even know where my father, mother, uncle, and aunt are buried.
SAMIR	Let go of me!

EDWARD rushes in to free SAMIR from AHMED.

EDWARD	Ahmed, what the hell is wrong with you?
AHMED	I had to beat him up.
EDWARD	He's a UN official.

AHMED	One good beating and he will forget all about the UN, Captain.
EDWARD	You have to obey American law here.
AHMED	I want American justice, Captain—beat him into silence!
EDWARD	*(ordering)* Sonic cannon!

A sonic cannon directs a thunderous boom at the gathered crowd.

AHMED	That's American justice? A sonic cannon? Give an order, Captain, give an order. If you don't want to, I'll give an order. I'll call FIF!
EDWARD	Nooo!
AHMED	Extra security?
EDWARD	I said no!
AHMED	Then what will you let me do, Captain?
EDWARD	Wait!
AHMED	For what?
EDWARD	This turmoil to turn into tragedy!

AHMED is hit by broken glass, his face bloodied. AHMED shows his newly injured face to EDWARD.

AHMED	This is a tragedy, Captain.
EDWARD	Go inside and clean the blood off your face. *(on satellite phone)* Code 662... I've got an injured staff member. Send medics in.

AHMED heads inside the compound. SAMIR and NAHLA step forward.

SAMIR	They can take her inside too!

The phone rings. EDWARD picks up and listens carefully.

EDWARD	Okay, I'll ask the mother, hang on.

(to NAHLA) Ma'am, does your daughter have a rare blood type?

NAHLA What happened?

EDWARD Do you know your daughter's blood type?

NAHLA Yes! O negative.

EDWARD *(into phone)* O negative.

EDWARD listens for a long time.

...Okay, thanks.

(to NAHLA) They don't have her blood type in stock.

NAHLA What happened to her?

EDWARD She needs a blood transfusion.

NAHLA Her father is O negative.

EDWARD What's his name?

NAHLA Omar...

EDWARD Omar what?

NAHLA Ahad.

EDWARD gets back on the phone.

EDWARD Lindsey, run a check on Omar Ahad.

NAHLA He's in jail.

EDWARD Why is he in jail?

SAMIR He's a poet.

EDWARD So?

SAMIR And a writer.

EDWARD All right, the poet is a writer, so? Why is he in jail?

SAMIR Saddam didn't like him.

EDWARD receives another call.

EDWARD *(into phone)* Find him.

(turning to NAHLA*)* Ma'am, your husband is a high-risk terrorist.

SAMIR	What did you say?
EDWARD	Her husband is a high-risk terrorist.
NAHLA	Terrorist, terrorist, terrorist... Okay, so he's a terrorist, so what? What difference does it make? He's locked up anyway. He's in an isolation cell! Away from everybody... away from the family... what can he do? Even a terrorist has a right to save his daughter, Captain. What did my daughter do? Why was she shot? Why are you holding her? She's wounded, and I cannot see her because her father is a terrorist? Nobody inside knows what to do with her. She needs her mother.
EDWARD	She needs blood more than her mother.
NAHLA	Okay, okay, I know what jail he's in.

EDWARD picks up the phone.

EDWARD	I've got someone on the line...

(into phone) Yes, I don't care. I command you to bring him... It's an order, Officer! Bring him in shackles or draw his blood in his cell... I don't care.

(to NAHLA*)* They have located him, ma'am.

We hear an ambulance pull into the compound.

(calling) Where is Ahmed? Ahmed, the ambulance is here for you.

NAHLA	Can't I go with him?
EDWARD	I told you...
NAHLA	But the ambulance is already here.
SAMIR	I'll okay this in my UN report...
NAHLA	Please, Captain... my child must be frightened.
EDWARD	I cannot let you in unless—
SAMIR	She's got a Canadian passport.

EDWARD	Do you, ma'am?
NAHLA	Yes!

She hands EDWARD her passport.

EDWARD	Ah... that's different.
NAHLA	Yes, I'm a Canadian. I would have been on a plane if my daughter hadn't been shot. I want to take her with me. That is why I am begging you.
EDWARD	I have rules to follow...
NAHLA	If something happens to her—
EDWARD	I understand.
NAHLA	Then let me go, please. All I want to do is hold her hand, bring her home, and head back to Canada. That's where she belongs. Do you want me to write it down?
EDWARD	Okay, okay. Go sit in the ambulance. I'll sign a special-entry pass for you.
NAHLA	You will?
SAMIR	*(overlapping with NAHLA)* You will?
EDWARD	Go!
NAHLA	Thank you, thank you, Captain.

NAHLA rushes towards the waiting ambulance with SAMIR following her.

Scene 4

One day later in HEKTOR's office. HEKTOR and EDWARD are in the middle of an argument.

HEKTOR   You ordered Omar Ahad to be brought to the army clinic?

EDWARD   To give blood, Commander!

HEKTOR   What's wrong with you?

EDWARD   He's the father of the girl.

HEKTOR   He is a high-risk terrorist.

EDWARD   He had the right blood type.

HEKTOR   He has blood on his hands.

EDWARD   This was a medical emergency...

HEKTOR   What if he escaped?

EDWARD is silent.

You let the mother through!

EDWARD   Because she feared the girl would die if—

HEKTOR   Are you going to trust anyone who gives you a story?

EDWARD   Commander, if the girl died while the mother was pleading at the checkpoint I would have had a bigger problem on my hands.

HEKTOR   The girl has died.

EDWARD   Now I'll have a real problem.

HEKTOR   And that's what you should take care of. There is some sheik dressed in biblical garb demonstrating his prowess to God. He's inciting a mob right outside the conference hall with the international media as witnesses. Stop this incident from becoming an embarrassment to us, Ed!

EDWARD   Yes, sir!

HEKTOR   You may go now.

EDWARD exits. HEKTOR picks up the phone.

I want all transcripts saved... I don't like what's going on... I said saved...

He puts down the phone as AHMED enters. He is bandaged and walks with slow, small steps.

HEKTOR	You're a good man and I'm glad you told me everything.
AHMED	It's my duty, sir.

HEKTOR looks at AHMED's bandaged face.

HEKTOR	You're hurt—
AHMED	I'm upset.
HEKTOR	About what?
AHMED	Her—
HEKTOR	Who?
AHMED	Why does she...?
HEKTOR	...?
AHMED	She... no.

He taps his head with his fist.

No, I better not—

HEKTOR	You don't start a conversation with me and leave it unfinished.
AHMED	What does the captain see in her?

He slaps his head with his fist.

No, I better not say anything... maybe there's garbage in my head.

HEKTOR	Empty the garbage, Ahmed.
AHMED	Captain has a soft heart for "other" women...

HEKTOR studies him, levelling a steady gaze at AHMED.

HEKTOR	Go on!

AHMED	I've seen him with the dark woman... I get a feeling Captain has a thing for *other* women. I know how nicely he treated Omar's wife—
HEKTOR	Well, she's got a Canadian passport.
AHMED	What is she doing here then? Why does she have more rights than Iraqis? She's not an Iraqi. Her husband is, but what good has he done for us? Why should Omar's Canadian wife get special treatment? Why did the captain listen to her and to that annoying UN guy who is half Canadian and half Iraqi? Why didn't he listen to me?
HEKTOR	...A full Iraqi!
AHMED	Right, sir! The captain humiliated me in front of him. In front of a half Iraqi who mocked my ancestors, teased me in the ambulance in front of Omar's wife. She looked at me as though I was the bad guy. He whispered something in her ear and she gave me a awful stare and looked away. I really wanted to spit on her face and beat him. He insulted me—he said I was working for the Americans.
HEKTOR	That's not an insult, Ahmed.
AHMED	Did I say something wrong?
HEKTOR	You'll be rewarded.

       AHMED exits.

Scene 5

OMAR's prison. NAHLA and OMAR are seen in the visiting room. They face each other with their heads down, but their conversation is clearly one of pain and loss. They stay facing each other for a long time.

OMAR   She said, "Baba, when you're free, can we go back to Canada?"

NAHLA   Now all that is left to take back is her dead body...

OMAR   What do you mean, Nahla?

A buzzer sounds, and AHMED takes OMAR back to his cell.

Scene 6

HEKTOR's office. A map is spread on the table. HEKTOR is talking to KENDRA.

KENDRA   Do we know why?

HEKTOR looks to the door.

HEKTOR   *(calling)* Ahmed!

AHMED enters and HEKTOR gestures for him to talk.

AHMED   Omar smuggled a message out, telling everyone that the dead girl was his daughter. His message was on the radio.

KENDRA   Was he able to?

AHMED   The sweeper is his informant.

HEKTOR   Now we have an insider on the prison staff.

AHMED holds up a notice for KENDRA.

AHMED   Omar accused Captain Edward. Iraqis are gathering from everywhere.

KENDRA   I don't care—I want to bring in new investors. I've got to rebuild Iraq contract by contract.

HEKTOR   You've got to neutralize men like Omar capture by capture.

EDWARD enters. He is surprised to see AHMED.

AHMED   *(surprised)* Oh, Captain, I was worried about you.

EDWARD   You should worry about the build-up at the checkpoint.

HEKTOR   You may go, Ahmed.

AHMED leaves. EDWARD watches him go with studying eyes.

EDWARD   What was he doing here?

HEKTOR   Nothing for you to worry about. He brought me the news of what's going on in the dead girl's case.

EDWARD   Okay.

Scene 7

A few weeks later. NAHLA is standing alone in an open field. SAMIR joins her.

NAHLA	No one is helping me.
SAMIR	No one knows how to!
NAHLA	Omar's uncle scolded me.
SAMIR	What did he say?
NAHLA	"If the soldiers were patrolling the streets, why did you let Ghazal go out?"
SAMIR	Sooner or later he will blame you for what happened to Omar.
NAHLA	He already does.
SAMIR	I have written to the Canadian ambassador.
NAHLA	I told him that the Americans have my daughter. He said, "Was she among the children taken in for stoning the army convoy?" I said, "No!" He said, "How could you be so sure?" I said, "Because my daughter was not arrested; she was shot dead."
SAMIR	What did he say to that?
NAHLA	He said, "Why didn't you leave when all the Canadians were flying back?"
SAMIR	Did you not tell him your husband is in jail?
NAHLA	He knows. And I told him I wanted to leave with Ghazal's body. He said her body is a complicated matter.
SAMIR	If our own government doesn't help us, I don't know who will.
NAHLA	That's what the sheik said.
SAMIR	Did you go to him?
NAHLA	He came to me.

SAMIR	At your house?
NAHLA	I am not a political animal. I'm an ordinary woman, but as a woman I know one thing: I didn't come to Iraq to have my child shot dead. That's not why I came here. I came for Omar, and now I'm stuck. I don't count for anything without him. I never did. All I had was my daughter and now I have nothing—he's in jail and she is gone. So if someone can help me get her body, I'll take it. I'll take her back to Canada and give her a proper funeral. At least there I have a family. The sheik promised he would get me the body.
SAMIR	The sheik is only interested in power.
NAHLA	That is why he will do something for me.

SHEIK enters. He gives SAMIR an unpleasant look.

SHEIK	Sister.
NAHLA	Sheik, they won't release her body.
SHEIK	They have no right to. But of course, given your husband's past—
NAHLA	My husband's past has become a problem.
SHEIK	Your husband's politics is the problem.
NAHLA	I have learned that the hard way.
SHEIK	First month in office the Butcher chased all godly men underground and paved the way for the evil imperialists to pound us. While the godless Butcher suppressed us, brother Omar rode through the city in open cars giving speeches that it was okay. Blasphemous speeches!
SAMIR	Blasphemous... they were not!
SHEIK	That explains why he's rotting in jail. The winds of our country change from time to time. And when they do, those without Allah one day become prisoners the next day. Don't teach me, Mr. UN!

SAMIR is silenced.

NAHLA   Sheik, all I ask you is to invoke the religious rite to claim
                  Ghazal's body.

SHEIK   It is my duty to help you. I have a plan for you, sister.
                  Come.

**SHEIK raises his hand as crowd noises start to rise.
An empty coffin is placed on stage as the noise of
the crowd grows. NAHLA starts to look surprised.
SHEIK motions, stopping the noise.**

SHEIK addresses the crowd.

Brothers, we are here because a little Iraqi girl who
blossomed in her parents' care has died. She grew to
love her family, her people, her religion, and her country.
She should have gone to school and grown to be a
woman, but instead a bullet shattered her head and
she died. Let me correct myself: she didn't die; she was
killed! Brothers, the Imperialists have kept her body
behind *(pointing)* that checkpoint. So touch this empty
coffin in her memory. We have gathered for the funeral
of thousands of little martyrs. *(pointing at NAHLA)* This
mother, the little martyr's mother—begged on her
knees... presented her papers... without arguments... just
begged the captain that the young girl needed a life-
saving blood transfusion, blood that could have come
from none other than her father.

SHEIK pulls out a family photograph of OMAR.

How happy she looks holding the hands of both her
parents. But the captain didn't believe her. How dare he
not believe a mother's call? Brothers, when I look at this
mother I feel an explosion of pride in my heart.

He turns his head towards the media.

Ladies and gentlemen of the press, please tell the world
what the Americans are doing to our people.

**The photographers' cameras click away amidst
journalists' questions.**

NAHLA   I had no idea—

SHEIK	*(to NAHLA)* Don't worry, good sister.

(to SAMIR) You—you, mister, I don't want to see you in the picture, move away...

SAMIR moves away.

(to NAHLA) I just want your picture holding your daughter's photo... hold it up a bit higher, a bit more...

NAHLA doesn't move but SHEIK pushes the picture higher towards her chest.

Now think of your child and point your fingers at the checkpoint.

She doesn't move again, but the SHEIK makes her do so.

Now, think of the captain who held you back at the checkpoint! Good, now, look at the photo and look at the checkpoint, one more time, again, again... and one more... Good.

(ordering media) Photos, please...

The cameras click again.

Great, that sure was radiant... Brothers, that captain did what he had to—now we have to do what *(pointing above)* Allah commands us to. In the name of the Almighty, I hereby order that the captain be handed over to us to face Allah's justice. Fatwa!

A roar rises among the crowd. SHEIK moves close to NAHLA.

NAHLA	I didn't want to be photographed.
SHEIK	Why? You have a beautiful face.
NAHLA	I didn't want to go public.
SHEIK	You were wise to, sister.
NAHLA	You offered me help.
SHEIK	I helped.

NAHLA	I asked for—
SHEIK	I gave a powerful eulogy.
NAHLA	Those weren't the words of a eulogy.
SHEIK	What could I say about a child's short life but that she died for Allah?
NAHLA	She died looking for her father.
SHEIK	Allah is the father of all.
SAMIR	But she was running to find her father... I have a transcript to prove it...
SHEIK	Oh, you keep your mouth shut.
NAHLA	She died in the war.
SHEIK	She died with honour.
SAMIR	Sheik, all that sister wants is the girl's body.
SHEIK	The body is nothing.
NAHLA	Don't say that.
SAMIR	The body is everything.
SHEIK	Justice is everything and I must get that for her.

SHEIK **brings out a headshot of** EDWARD **and presses it into** NAHLA**'s hand.**

This face will be on every street corner.

SHEIK **exits.** NAHLA **and** SAMIR **watch as the crowd leaves, following** SHEIK. NAHLA **folds the headshot.**

NAHLA	The captain helped me.
SAMIR	Yeah, but the sheik wants Allah to help you.
NAHLA	Fatwa isn't Allah's work.
SAMIR	Just last week, sister, the sheik gave a speech at another child's funeral. He loves funerals. The sheik spoke about God and God-haters, believers and non-believers. The crowd went crazy. Men beat their chests in praise of

Allah, and attacked an army convoy with their bare hands. They burned down an entire neighbourhood...

NAHLA   Now Omar will be mad.

SAMIR   Because you didn't get the body?

NAHLA	Because I went to the sheik!
SAMIR	*(with a studying stare)* But the sheik is not your real problem.
NAHLA	You just said the opposite a minute ago.
SAMIR	It's what's between Omar and Commander Hektor...
NAHLA	There is nothing between them.
SAMIR	Why do you think the commander didn't let Omar give blood?

NAHLA **stares at him questioningly.**

Don't tell me Omar didn't tell you.

NAHLA	Didn't tell me what?
SAMIR	Everyone knows there were issues between Omar and the commander... issues from the past!
NAHLA	Issues from the past are beside the point to me.
SAMIR	Issues from the past are exactly the reason why the commander is not releasing the body.
NAHLA	I cannot pick a fight with the commander.
SAMIR	If you could tell me a little bit more, something more than what people are whispering, something that is uniquely from you, I could get Hektor's attention. Maybe then I could bargain with him. Some give and take and you may get her body.
NAHLA	If I knew something, I would tell you.
SAMIR	You're hiding something from me.
NAHLA	All I knew I told the captain—you heard that.

NAHLA **walks away.** SAMIR **follows.**

Scene 8

KENDRA's quarters. KENDRA is buttoning her blouse as EDWARD starts to get dressed.

KENDRA	Is something wrong?
EDWARD	Have to see Hektor. Back to the checkpoint.
KENDRA	What time is it?
EDWARD	Doesn't matter.
KENDRA	There is a fatwa against you.
EDWARD	There is a fatwa against every American.
KENDRA	But it's your mug shot that's on every lamppost.
EDWARD	What do you want me to do? Go into hiding? Change my appearance?
KENDRA	Hektor is very worried.
EDWARD	He's worried about Omar the terrorist!
KENDRA	I'm worried about terrorists. I am also worried about Omar. What if his girl's death discourages investors?
EDWARD	What if the girl hadn't died?
KENDRA	You're feeling guilty!
EDWARD	What if—
KENDRA	What if, what if, what if... what if there wasn't a war, but there is—
EDWARD	So everything goes.
KENDRA	What is happening to you, Ed?
EDWARD	Why won't Hektor release the girl's body?
KENDRA	Because that would be newsworthy and make the war look bad.
EDWARD	Well, that doesn't make me feel any better.

KENDRA   Well, it will make me feel better if you didn't go out at this hour. If you take my advice, don't take on Hektor!

EDWARD   Don't worry.

Scene 9

SAMIR visits HEKTOR's office. We catch them in mid-conversation.

SAMIR   The UN has authorized me to reopen Ahad's file.

HEKTOR   What's going on?

SAMIR   Omar asked his wife to—

HEKTOR   To do what?

SAMIR   Approach conference delegates.

HEKTOR   Why?

SAMIR   She has made a deposition in Omar's name.

HEKTOR   Saying what?

SAMIR   Your name appears in it several times.

HEKTOR   Because I take care of terrorists personally!

SAMIR   Your relationship with Omar goes way back—way before the war!

HEKTOR   He was already in jail before the war.

SAMIR   1979?

HEKTOR   1991!

SAMIR   War before that.

HEKTOR   What war was that?

SAMIR   1980!

HEKTOR   The Iran–Iraq war?

SAMIR   So many wars, it's hard to keep track of... right, Commander!

HEKTOR   Let's skip the history.

SAMIR   You had an audience with Omar Ahad during the Iran–Iraq war.

HEKTOR   I have audiences with heads of state—so?

SAMIR   So why is he in jail?

HEKTOR   He had issues with the Butcher.

SAMIR   The Butcher is gone! Why is he still in jail?

HEKTOR   Ask the prime minister.

SAMIR   There was a secret pact made between you and Omar.

HEKTOR   Is that what Omar told you?

SAMIR   The conference countries want to know. Commander, I need access to old documents. I need to speak to your staff that I deem necessary. I will speak with the prime minister to get to the bottom of the issue. I need to speak to Captain Alston. He will be required to give me a written statement of what happened that day. And you'll be required to speak to me under oath.

HEKTOR   I think we are done.

> **SAMIR continues talking, but HEKTOR ignores him and escorts him to the door.**

Scene 10

HEKTOR visits OMAR in jail. OMAR is summoned to the interrogation room. AHMED waits outside but is visible.

HEKTOR   What did you tell that UN man?

OMAR   Not everything!

HEKTOR   Don't forget who you are, Omar! Remember Widad?

OMAR   The man who struck his enemies with an axe!

HEKTOR   Why didn't he axe you in the head?

OMAR   I don't know.

HEKTOR   Because I took him out. Thanks to me you're still alive. Remember the men we saved from him?

OMAR   My friends.

HEKTOR   They are speaking out. You double-crossed them.

OMAR   You double-crossed me!

HEKTOR   You're a liar, and your lies are causing a problem for the conference.

OMAR   The conference of warlords and capitalists?

HEKTOR   They are rebuilding the country.

OMAR   Let them see my wife's deposition.

HEKTOR   Okay, Omar, according to that deposition, you have proof that implicates me.

OMAR   You know that.

HEKTOR   Nothing that worries me, but it has become a nuissance. Officially, I can let the prime minister loose on you. But, unofficially, we can negotiate.

OMAR   With what?

HEKTOR   I've got your daughter. And your wife wants to take her body out.

OMAR	Leave my family alone.
HEKTOR	Family is everything, Omar. You hand over those documents and I will hand you back your daughter's body.
OMAR	Do you think I would swap your secret for my daughter's corpse?

HEKTOR walks away from him and calls for AHMED.

Ahmed...

AHMED	Yes, Commander.
HEKTOR	What do we do to a dog that bites?
AHMED	You know better.
HEKTOR	I want to hear it.
AHMED	We rattle...
HEKTOR	Rattle what?
AHMED	His brain!
HEKTOR	Inside this prison?
AHMED	Inside his skull...
HEKTOR	Why his skull?
AHMED	Because it leaves no external marks.
HEKTOR	Take him in.

AHMED puts a restraining jacket on OMAR and pushes him into the interrogation chamber. We hear OMAR's painful screams. HEKTOR covers his ears and AHMED looks away. Lights fade out to complete darkness and then fade back in. We see HEKTOR sitting in his office in the dark.

Scene 11

EDWARD	Why are you sitting in the dark?

HEKTOR turns a light on.

HEKTOR	I'm stressed.
EDWARD	Who isn't?
HEKTOR	Kendra tells me you're feeling weird.
EDWARD	What's bothering you, Commander?
HEKTOR	Do you want to be a hero?
EDWARD	No, sir.

HEKTOR lifts a file folder from his desk.

HEKTOR	Good, I don't like heroes. There are hundreds of wannabe heroes inside this file. Here's one.

He pulls out a page and reads.

"The greatest enemies of America aren't in Baghdad— they are in the White House, who have sent us to kill or die."

EDWARD reaches for the file.

EDWARD	Who is this hero?

HEKTOR pounds his hand on the file.

HEKTOR	The hero has since withdrawn his statement. Do you want to withdraw yours?
EDWARD	I never wrote one.
HEKTOR	Good, then don't. An army lawyer will write one for you.
EDWARD	What are we talking about?
HEKTOR	We have a problem, Ed. The UN has launched an inquiry and you're expected to give a written statement. The army lawyer will write that for you.
EDWARD	I can write it myself.

EDWARD	And the UN pain-in-the-butt Samir will ask you questions—I don't want *him* talking to you.
EDWARD	Why?
HEKTOR	Because he is Omar's man, and Omar wants revenge.
EDWARD	I tried to help Omar's daughter.
HEKTOR	That doesn't change Omar. You've become his target. Samir is doing everything for Omar's release. And believe me, you don't want to be seen at the checkpoint when the terrorist Omar comes out.
EDWARD	Why should he come after me?
HEKTOR	You stopped his wife at the checkpoint.
EDWARD	I didn't—you did.
HEKTOR	But he's after you... not me!

The phone rings. HEKTOR picks it up and listens.

Call from the president, I've got to take it...

HEKTOR rushes off. EDWARD picks up the file and opens it, shuffles through it quickly, pulls out some pages, and stuffs them in his pocket. HEKTOR turns back to EDWARD.

HEKTOR	I'm removing you from the checkpoint.
EDWARD	Why?
HEKTOR	It's my job to protect you. You'll be under watch 24-7.

HEKTOR picks up the folder and leaves. EDWARD pulls the pages he had stolen from the file, studies them, puts them back in his pocket, and leaves.

Scene 12

NAHLA visits OMAR in prison. NAHLA and OMAR speak through the metal bars of his cell.

NAHLA   How long can you go on like this?

OMAR   They've done a good job this time.

NAHLA   You haven't slept.

OMAR   I tried.

NAHLA   Are you eating well?

OMAR   Are you?

NAHLA   You must eat, Omar!

OMAR   It's not that I'm not eating, just that I don't feel like eating.

NAHLA   Why is God punishing us?

OMAR   Where is he? I prayed, Nahla, for the first time in my life I prayed. I prayed for Ghazal. I prayed for the children killed in this war.

Silence.

Does anybody remember how many children have died in the war?

NAHLA   You weren't there when Ghazal died.

OMAR   You don't know how much I wanted to come home to her. I wanted to hold her in these arms. I wanted to read my words to her. They are punishing us, punishing us through our children.

NAHLA   I'm frightened. When I see a child in the street, I want to tell her mother, lock her up. Don't let her out. Don't let her get shot.

OMAR   What is your family saying in Canada?

NAHLA   They want me to come back.

OMAR   Why don't you?

NAHLA   I want to take you with me.

OMAR   I'm not free.

NAHLA   Samir says your release will come soon.

OMAR   How will my leaving solve anything?

NAHLA   How will you staying in jail solve anything?

OMAR   I know, Nahla. I know it has been years of separation; I long for your love, your kisses, and your touch.

NAHLA   I can't go on living on your words alone.

OMAR   I write about you every day.

NAHLA   I can't live on your poetry delivered to me by a prison guard.

OMAR   This will change.

NAHLA   My world has changed since Ghazal's death.

OMAR   Ghazal's death will change the fate of Iraq... let me tell you that.

NAHLA   Your changing Iraq has taken our daughter from us.

OMAR   You're blaming me.

NAHLA   And I must beg for the release of her body!

OMAR   Do you know why they are not releasing her body?

NAHLA   Do you want to know why she died in the first place?

OMAR   Yes, yes, yes... I know, I know, I know—

NAHLA   Where are those documents?

         OMAR **turns away from her.**

         They raided our house for your documents. The soldier ordered me to go down on my hands and knees and look under the bed. I said I wanted to call the Canadian embassy. And Commander Hektor said, "First you're going to write down everything about your husband—his friends, his family, his comrades, and where he's hiding his documents." He forced a pen and paper into my hand.

OMAR's mood is beginning to change.

OMAR	Nahla, what did you write?
NAHLA	He said, "Swear by your daughter and write the truth and we will let you call the Canadian embassy."
OMAR	What did you write?
NAHLA	What could I write, Omar? I said, "I'm telling the truth; I don't know where my husband keeps his documents"!
OMAR	Good.
NAHLA	And then Ghazal said, "If I ask my father where he keeps them will you let my mother go?" He said yes! And she ran out. Then I waited for her to return to the checkpoint, and she did not.
OMAR	That captain will pay.
NAHLA	The captain helped me. Don't think of taking revenge on him.
OMAR	I promise...
NAHLA	No revenge for Ghazal.
OMAR	Revenge for the thousands of Ghazals.
NAHLA	There goes your promise.
OMAR	I want my child back.
NAHLA	We can't have our child back... but maybe... just maybe we can save what is left of her.
OMAR	How?
NAHLA	Hand Hektor's secret back to him and he will give us Ghazal's body.
OMAR	I'm not bargaining with her body.
NAHLA	You think that's bargaining?

OMAR	She's my call for freedom.
NAHLA	Omar, she is gone.
OMAR	She lives. She lives inside of me.
NAHLA	She lives in a morgue. I need to take her from there and rest her soul, have a proper funeral in Canada.
OMAR	You can't take her body out of the country.
NAHLA	I will, Omar.
OMAR	She's a daughter of this land.
NAHLA	She's the daughter of this mother.
OMAR	And I am her father.
NAHLA	The father can join her. Samir is working for your release. I have already submitted an affidavit.
OMAR	What did you fill in?
NAHLA	Retraction of my decision to stay back, to pledge peace, and not engage in politics!
OMAR	You'll do that so you can leave?
NAHLA	I live in the house I lived in with Ghazal. I cannot bear it alone—without her.
OMAR	You can't leave with that kind of pledge, no!

NAHLA is stunned with disbelief. An alarm sounds and NAHLA starts to walk away.

And you can't take her body out of Iraq.

NAHLA	I will.

NAHLA walks away. OMAR is led away.

Scene 13

The PRIME MINISTER's office.

PRIME MINISTER	The man is on trial for treason.
SAMIR	He's there without a trial.
PRIME MINISTER	Could you repeat that?
SAMIR	And when a terrorist is in prison without trial, everyone knows what's going on.
PRIME MINISTER	Repeat that again!
SAMIR	Someone is killing the opposition. Conference delegates have seen the bodies—blindfolded, handcuffed, gouged out eyeballs...
PRIME MINISTER	I haven't seen any.
SAMIR	And they will not tolerate if something happened to Omar.
PRIME MINISTER	Omar, Omar, Omar—
SAMIR	The fact is he has become a political curiosity for the countries at the table.
PRIME MINISTER	What happened to George Bush's road map?
SAMIR	Nobody gives a fig about George Bush's road map. But please, don't forget that the delegates and the investors are accountable to their citizens back home. They are asking why Omar is still in jail, and why his daughter's body is not released.
PRIME MINISTER	That is because of Hektor Frank.
SAMIR	But you're the prime minister, not Hektor Frank.
PRIME MINISTER	Quite right.
SAMIR	You are risking being perceived as a proxy prime minister.
PRIME MINISTER	Okay, okay, here is what I'll do. I'll have Omar moved from prison to house arrest.

SAMIR   But it's the girl's body...

PRIME MINISTER   The girl's body later. But for now, give Omar the good news—prime minister as I am, I'm releasing him from jail to a house arrest.

SAMIR   You must want something in return.

PRIME MINISTER   He will keep his mouth shut, and not engage in anything disruptive.

SAMIR   I'll take that.

SAMIR shakes the prime minister's hand and leaves, content with the outcome.

Scene 14

KENDRA's home in Baghdad. EDWARD is reading documents. KENDRA is typing on her laptop.

EDWARD
(reading) Listen to this one: "I was explicitly told that I could shoot anyone who did not immediately move when I ordered them to do so, keeping in mind I don't speak Arabic."

KENDRA
Ed, I'm trying to work here—I got a phone call from Washington...

EDWARD
"And my commander told me that our mission was"— and I quote—"to kill those who need to be killed and save those who need to be saved"...

KENDRA
What are you reading?

EDWARD
Soldiers' reports!

KENDRA
What do you mean?

EDWARD
I was in his office and he was angry. He made me listen to a statement from a file and said, "This private wants to be a hero like you." He said the private was unfit for the army. He asked if I wanted to be a hero. Before I could say anything, he got a call from the president and left the room. My eyes froze on the file. The title read *Soldiers in Need of Attention*. I got curious and suspicious. Something came over me. I opened the file and grabbed a handful of pages from it and stuffed them into my pocket. I have never done anything like that in my life, but that night—

KENDRA
You stole classified papers?

EDWARD
Yes!

KENDRA
My God!

EDWARD
It was worth it.

KENDRA
Jesus Christ! Are you proud of yourself?

EDWARD
One soldier wrote the army had pulled an entire family

out of their car and ordered the father down on his knees to beg in front of his children. He was kicked in front of his kids. Another one wrote...

KENDRA   Ed, you're in breach of the rules.

EDWARD   And then I started going around talking to the boys—

KENDRA   You're organizing them?

EDWARD   I'm telling them we came here to defend our flag, but we are killing people and lying to the world.

KENDRA   You will be disciplined, Ed.

EDWARD   Those files were meant to be destroyed after the army fixed them up.

KENDRA   What does that mean?

EDWARD   The boys were made to change their statements.

KENDRA   How?

EDWARD   The "killings" were changed to "incidents."

KENDRA   You don't understand.

EDWARD   I don't understand what?

KENDRA   Hektor will be pissed off. Really pissed off.

EDWARD   The army has written a statement for me that says the girl wasn't *killed*, that it was an *incident*. He wants me to sign that statement. If I did, it would be a cover-up. I signed some of those cover-ups before, but now I know the truth.

KENDRA   What is it between you and the Ahad family?

EDWARD   Nothing.

KENDRA   Why are you so dutiful to them?

EDWARD   I don't even know them personally.

KENDRA   Then why are you standing up to the army for them?

EDWARD   I just want to do the right thing.

KENDRA   Ed, you're still a captain in the army. You can change all
            these things—

EDWARD   Kendra, her eyes were still open. After she died, no one
            bothered to close them. Because everyone was busy
            covering it up. I can't forget her. I can't forget she was
            looking at me with her opened eyes.

KENDRA   Ed, in war these things happen...

EDWARD   When I first came here, I thought I could do this job
            decently.

KENDRA   It's an honourable job, Ed.

EDWARD   And I'm not ashamed to say that I helped that mother.

KENDRA   It's more than helping that mother.

EDWARD   I know the army wants to make everything look good in
            the eyes of the world... but it doesn't make me feel good
            about myself.

KENDRA   The army will court-martial you.

EDWARD   So be it.

            KENDRA kisses him then gathers her things.

KENDRA   You are a good man, but a confused one. I can talk to
            you but right now I have to get to the conference. But I
            want you to think about it again.

            She leaves.

Scene 15

> OMAR is home, under his house arrest. He is writing.
> NAHLA approaches him with suspicion.

NAHLA	What are you writing?
OMAR	My speech for the conference.
NAHLA	Have you forgotten the condition of your release? Already?
OMAR	I didn't agree to any conditions, Samir did.
NAHLA	So you'll put Samir in danger.
OMAR	He can handle it.
NAHLA	You said the conference was illegal.
OMAR	But I want them to invite me.
NAHLA	Why would they invite you?
OMAR	If they don't, something will happen.
NAHLA	Buses will be blown up?
OMAR	It's a strategy, Nahla...
NAHLA	It's terrorism!
OMAR	It's business!
NAHLA	Business?
OMAR	If our boys blow up a couple of buses, abort the conference, and get shot by soldiers, America will see that on CNN and feel bad because in their minds their soldiers have gone to fight the evil, not to shoot civilians.
NAHLA	And you will let boys be sacrificed for a fifteen-second clip on CNN!
OMAR	Yes! I mean no! But I have got to do whatever—
NAHLA	Even if that endangers the release of Ghazal's body—
OMAR	She is a martyr.

NAHLA	Are you using her name in your speech?
OMAR	She is my daughter.
NAHLA	You can't use her name...
OMAR	Nahla, listen...
NAHLA	No, you listen. Ghazal was not a martyr. She was an innocent girl who died in a war she had nothing to do with. I want to remember her for her innocence. I don't want you to use her name for your cause.
OMAR	You hurt me.
NAHLA	You've hurt us all.
OMAR	She's my daughter.
NAHLA	I forbid you from using her name. I want you to leave my daughter out of it. I want peace for my daughter...

OMAR gets up and walks away. NAHLA takes a deep breath and walks up to him. She presents him a long form that bears the insignia of the Canadian federal government.

	I don't know what is happening to us.
OMAR	Nothing can happen.
NAHLA	I'm sorry.
OMAR	I'm sorry too...
NAHLA	Don't let this ordeal destroy us.
OMAR	Yes!
NAHLA	Let's save what we have of us.
OMAR	We must.
NAHLA	I want you to cooperate.

OMAR becomes suddenly tense.

OMAR	What do you want me to do?
NAHLA	Don't say no to this.

OMAR   Don't ask me to go into exile!

NAHLA   Canada is not your exile, it's our home.

OMAR   It is your home. Everything I want is here.

NAHLA   Think beyond yourself, Omar.

OMAR   I always think about others.

NAHLA   Think about me, think about Ghazal, and stop this drama.

OMAR   Drama? You think it's drama? Huh?

(dramatically) I need to call out to my people, "C'mon, brothers, c'mon, sisters, let's turn our joys, our laments, and our prayers into rage against the enemy. Let's make history." Things don't happen on their own, Nahla; we make them happen. How can I dare pass up a chance to make things happen? Do you know?

NAHLA   You can make all the drama you want, read all the poetry you ever wrote, and take all the curtain calls you can get, but you'll have no audience because Hektor will send you back to jail. Do you not fear what they will do to you? To us?

OMAR   I don't fear anyone in my mission to save my country.

NAHLA   You couldn't save your own daughter, Omar—wake up.

OMAR   I'm so proud of her.

NAHLA   I just don't understand you. I don't understand a father who loses his child and feels proud...

OMAR   You don't understand.

NAHLA   No, you don't understand—I'll go back. And I'm asking you to come with me.

OMAR   What will people remember of me? That I fled while my people were fighting for freedom. How do you think that will make me feel?

NAHLA	That's just it, Omar. It's all about you. Have you ever thought about how it makes me feel to have left my home and my family behind for a man who loves his cause more than me?

Silence.

There is nothing left for me here.

OMAR	It's our home.
NAHLA	It's your home. My home is in Canada. In your home I will live childless and grow old looking out the kitchen window while you fight for the freedom of your people looking out your cell window.
OMAR	You've plunged a knife in my chest.
NAHLA	You have no love for me.
OMAR	That's not true.
NAHLA	You have no love for Ghazal.
OMAR	You're hurting me.
NAHLA	Revenge is all you know. But revenge is not going to give us back our daughter.
OMAR	I would want no revenge from anyone if I can get my daughter back. But I can't have her, can I? At least I'm in my country to remember her.
NAHLA	There is no country, Omar. The country is dead. Why do you think people are leaving their family homes in the middle of the night? There is no country. Why do you think I went down on my knees in front of that commander? Why do you think I begged the captain? There is no country. The country killed our daughter, it is killing me, and it will kill you. You have to think of your family... or what is left of your family... not your country.
OMAR	I can't leave without fighting the fight.
NAHLA	I can't go on living like that.

OMAR   What did you say?

NAHLA   Just what you heard. I can't go on living like that.

           OMAR is stunned. NAHLA exits.

Scene 16

Army headquarters. HEKTOR is questioning EDWARD. He slides a document in front of EDWARD.

HEKTOR   The lawyers have cleaned up your statement, Ed!

EDWARD reads the document.

EDWARD   This is not what happened.

HEKTOR   That's exactly what happened.

EDWARD   The lawyers omitted a crucial truth.

HEKTOR   They omitted a crucial truth because it was the truth—so fucking what? The fact is it will protect you.

EDWARD   The girl died in our custody.

HEKTOR   If I could bring her back to life I'd—but the dead don't come back. But if you accept the lawyer's version, I can save you from court-martial—that's what I am doing.

EDWARD   I don't know, sir...

HEKTOR   Let me tell you one last time, Captain—this statement is issued by the US Army. This represents you and me—loyalty, God, the flag, and the country.

EDWARD   What about the truth? I can't lie about this one. I won't lie about the girl and her mother.

HEKTOR   The Canadian government recalled all of its citizens. Why didn't she go back?

EDWARD   Why aren't you letting her go?

HEKTOR   Why did she let her ten-year-old run towards the restricted zone?

EDWARD   Do you think she gave birth to a child to have her shot dead?

HEKTOR   We do our best to avoid the innocent.

EDWARD   But the innocent get in the way—

HEKTOR	Don't talk rubbish, Ed.
EDWARD	I want to be excused... sir!
HEKTOR	Go!

EDWARD starts to leave.

Ed...

EDWARD stops.

One more thing. If you are found talking to the press—or your girlfriend, boyfriend, father, mother, cousin, or second cousin—you'll be in trouble. Don't throw away twenty years of army service, Captain—guilt is not a practical sentiment for a soldier.

EDWARD leaves.

Scene 17

AHMED and the SHEIK at an unidentified location.

SHEIK Kill those who obstruct the Kingdom.

AHMED By the pleasure of paradise...

The SHEIK hands him a bundle of paper money. AHMED counts it.

SHEIK You are receiving from the Americans, aren't you?

AHMED Sheik, the government has given my ancestral land to someone who has not lived in this city. This is no justice.

SHEIK When man's justice is so corrupt, you must look to His justice *(points upwards)*. Here is some extra.

He gives him a tight bundle of US dollars. AHMED exits.

The lights dim. The SHEIK starts to walk away when his cellphone rings.

Yes, of course. I will personally take care of it. Yes, tomorrow. My men know the procedure. The conference will open with some nice fireworks. Yes, I've got the list in my hand. Number six is a priority. His family is trying to smuggle him out of the country. Yes, yes, I will deal with him myself. Yes, in the same place? And the same amount in Euros. We agreed for my family in France.

Good, good.

Salaam alaikum.

The SHEIK looks around surreptitiously, and exits cautiously, avoiding being seen by anyone.

Scene 18

> A bar in the American enclave. KENDRA is sipping a drink as EDWARD arrives. She is reading a newspaper article that features a picture of GHAZAL's mock funeral.

KENDRA You refused to fix your statement.

EDWARD Yes.

KENDRA Hektor was trying to protect you.

EDWARD He is trying to protect himself.

KENDRA Ed, if you want to desert the army—

EDWARD I want to tell the truth.

KENDRA The truth is our boys are dying in this war. There was an army salute for this twenty-four-year-old who was blown up right outside the conference. Tears were rolling down the eyes of the privates carrying his coffin. It was on TV. The flags, the flowers the ribbons... Maybe you didn't see but there were many teary eyes in America.

EDWARD Were there teary eyes for this girl? Did anybody even see what happened to her? Did the TV cameras go to shoot the school she went to or the park she played in? Did anybody write a card for her? Do the folks in America know why her mother was crying before me?

KENDRA Ed, that was an accident.

EDWARD And what Hektor is doing after the "accident" is also an accident, is it?

KENDRA You want to take on Hektor.

EDWARD I want to tell the truth.

KENDRA You're accusing America.

EDWARD I'm accusing Hektor.

KENDRA	Accusing Hektor is accusing America!
EDWARD	People back home have the right to know.

     EDWARD exits.

Scene 19

EDWARD and **SAMIR**, with camera equipment, approach **OMAR**'s safe house. **SAMIR** encourages **EDWARD** to go ahead to the door, and he hides himself. **NAHLA** answers. She is stunned to see **EDWARD**.

NAHLA	My husband is inside.
EDWARD	I've come to see him.
NAHLA	He will kill you.
EDWARD	Ma'am, I've something to tell you.
NAHLA	Please go.
EDWARD	Where?
NAHLA	Back to your country, I guess, just go.
OMAR *(offstage)*	Who is it?
NAHLA	Nobody...
OMAR	Has he got a name?
NAHLA	*(to OMAR)* Just a minute...
	(to EDWARD) Please, disappear...

She touches his arm.

Save yourself from him. I'm closing the door.

OMAR enters.

OMAR	No, don't.
EDWARD	I'm the captain from the checkpoint. Hello!
OMAR	Hello... you're sweating...
EDWARD	I guess.
OMAR	My wife has been telling me that you tried to help her.
EDWARD	And if she hadn't told you that?
OMAR	I would have squeezed your neck with my bare hands.

EDWARD	I believe you.
OMAR	You shouldn't. I have never killed anyone in my life, but my politics have given me the reputation of a killer.
EDWARD	I don't want to be seen talking to you.
OMAR	Come in.

EDWARD enters at OMAR's invitation and SAMIR steps forward with his camera equipment.

NAHLA	Oh! So it's you who's behind this.

SAMIR shows her his camera equipment.

SAMIR	They will be on film. And they will talk

As SAMIR is setting up his camera, EDWARD and OMAR sit down side by side, facing the camera for the shoot.

Rolling... start.

NAHLA	As if I didn't even exist.

We see OMAR and EDWARD's lips move, but we don't hear them.

Scene 20

The Conference for Democracy and the Salvation of Iraq. The delegates and investors are already seated in the background.

AHMED is guarding the conference gates and performing a security check of some of the delegates. SAMIR enters and sets up his camera equipment.

AHMED

Come, everyone. Come to the Conference for Democracy and the Salvation of Iraq. Welcome, delegates, welcome. Go that way, you'll see the sign Small Business Subcontracting, go past that. Look for army girls in miniskirts and T-shirts... take an information package from them. Go through the second security point, go past the prime minister's thinking room, go past President George Bush's wall photo, and there you'll find the European room on the left, the American room on the right, and the Arab room right in the middle. Not hard at all to find it.

KENDRA enters with the PRIME MINISTER. SAMIR stops him for an interview, but HEKTOR intervenes.

HEKTOR

Are you going to do this interview?

PRIME MINISTER

I always do interviews.

HEKTOR

Save it for later.

KENDRA

To the podium, Mr. Prime Minister...

He steps up to the podium.

PRIME MINISTER

My friends, the birth of a country is like the birth of a child—nature puts the mother through labour pains, but when the baby is born everybody is happy. So thank you, investors, thank you, willing governments, thank you all for inducing labour pains in mother Iraq, for now a new country is about to be born.

KENDRA

Dear valued investors, you are helping the prime minister build a democracy in Iraq that will give you new markets in the Middle East.

As KENDRA and the PRIME MINISTER speak, outside the checkpoint we see OMAR in shadow and can hear his speech on a radio. The focus shifts to OMAR.

OMAR

I am speaking to all Iraqis and to the people of the world. I am asking you to give us a voice, and I want you to see the truth. I ask you to ask them—those in the conference—where are the Iraqis?

Murmurs and questioning noises rise from the crowd.

The focus shifts back to the PRIME MINISTER.

PRIME MINISTER

Iraqis have returned from exile to rebuild our nation, and I have a plan for them. I've a road map that is engraved on the palm of my hand.

He splays his fingers and closes them into a fist, one by one, as he goes on.

Infrastructure, raw material, export-import, health and education, oil fields. Did you know Iraq has the second largest oil reserve in the world? That's below ground! I'm here to tell you what's above ground: twenty-five million hard-working Iraqis who want to roll up their sleeves and build a new Iraq.

Outside, OMAR's speech continues.

OMAR

Brothers and sisters, they came to destroy weapons of mass destruction and destroyed our country. They killed my daughter. My only daughter. I'll never see my Ghazal. But let me tell you, as a father, I don't long only for my daughter, but for the thousands of daughters whose lives have been cut short by this war. Brothers and sisters, let's transform the deaths of each of our children into a call for the *real* rebuilding of our country.

A roar of joy.

The crowd goes crazy. Sounds of explosions.

PRIME MINISTER

Dear friends, terrorists hate trade. But you can bid them

farewell with your contract bids.

A gentle applause from the investors and delegates.

KENDRA Ladies and gentlemen, thirteen billion dollars worth of contracts are to be auctioned off: 1,100 building projects, sixty-seven clinics, fifteen hospitals, eighty-three railroads, two hundred highways, and twenty-two power plants.

PRIME MINISTER And for the first time in Iraq in six thousand years, an indoor flush toilet for every household. Bids are open for toilets.

KENDRA Thank you, Mr. Prime Minister... Thank you so much.

Mild laugher among the investors.

OMAR Don't get me wrong. I thank investors, I thank contractors... thank you. We welcome you to our country. We thank you for coming to rebuild Iraq.

PRIME MINISTER The terrorists are trying to misguide you with their cunning and their cruelty.

OMAR I ask the people and the countries of this conference: Do you want to sign a contract with blood money?

PRIME MINISTER I ask you, investors: Do you want to go back without signing contracts?

OMAR But ask before signing anything. Where are the children? What is happening to them? What happened to my daughter? Why has her body not been given back to us.

PRIME MINISTER We are on a march for democracy. My country is open for business. Make your bids, ladies and gentlemen, make your bids.

KENDRA starts the auction, the PRIME MINISTER repeats after her.

KENDRA Construction—building project, one million dollar building project, starting at one million dollars.

PRIME MINISTER Anyone for two million...

KENDRA   Looking for the first bidder, one million start value...

PRIME MINISTER   Two million... start value... Bid on, ladies and gentlemen, bid on, $550 million smells pretty good—you don't want to flush an opportunity like this down the toilet...

Their auctioning fades into the next scene.

Scene 21

> KENDRA's Baghdad home. EDWARD is sitting as KENDRA enters and kisses him in greeting. He responds coldly.

KENDRA You missed the "eloquence" of the prime minister.

EDWARD A million dollars of eloquence was sitting in the closet...

KENDRA What are you talking about?

> EDWARD drops a bag of cash on the floor.

EDWARD What's this?

KENDRA Why... Where did you—

EDWARD A million dollars in cash—

KENDRA You put that back!

EDWARD Where did it come from?

KENDRA Okay, it's the ambassador's emergency fund.

EDWARD How many more millions are in the closet?

KENDRA Ed, this is for designated agents! Don't tell me you didn't pay Iraqis who spied for you.

EDWARD I paid *them*.

KENDRA Okay, so I kept some for me. Does it break your little heart?

EDWARD How long has this been going on?

KENDRA We've been bribing the locals since the war started. For God's sake, we've been bribing heads of state... How do you think we got all those warlords and exiles to the conference?

EDWARD Puff up their pockets, but what the heck, let me help myself first.

KENDRA They were going to burn it, Ed.

EDWARD What?

KENDRA	The cash, millions and millions of dollars, tons of it— you'd need a crane to move it—the army was going to burn it.
EDWARD	What?
KENDRA	What does burn mean? They burn the money so there's no trace. What do you think they do with the fund for underground activity? Put it in an audit statement? "One thousand dollars for mercenaries, two thousand for informers, ten thousand for stuffing ballot boxes, twenty thousand for sending ministers' children abroad... Do you think the defence department would report an expense like that? So, the ambassador sent a soldier around to collect unused funds for incineration. And I told him to leave it in my closet.
EDWARD	And what if he reports you?
KENDRA	He stuffed his own pockets.
EDWARD	So that's what's going on?
	Beat.
KENDRA	God, I didn't want to say this—and I don't know how to—but I am a black woman—
EDWARD	You're a powerful black woman.
KENDRA	I'm the public face of the white America that the world doesn't trust.
EDWARD	You're talking about trust?
KENDRA	I've worked my ass off for this position, but in truth, America just uses me as a black woman who is a trustworthy alibi because she is a descendent of a slave. She will never risk the reputation of black America, and never step out of line.
EDWARD	Therefore she must steal?
KENDRA	Therefore you must understand. I have assembled investors and allied countries that no one in Washington would have been able to. Why would I take this

mammoth task on? Out of pure love for white America? I did this for one hope: that Iraq would rise up and that my accomplishments would be an example for black America. This little miscellaneous cash from the war zone is nothing compared to the big corruption in Washington. But if the corruption goes public, the investors and governments will go back home, and with that goes any chance the Iraqis have of a dignified life.

EDWARD Of course a dignified life means a cut of the purse for a poor black woman.

KENDRA Ed, what difference does it make if I kept some? It was going to be for us.

EDWARD I don't want a cent of it.

Beat.

KENDRA Who do you think you are, Ed? Do you think you're clean? You've spied on Hektor; you stole classified papers from his desk; you visited a terrorist who wants to destroy America—and you have the gall to accuse me?

EDWARD **starts to leave.**

Come back, Ed. I never thought I would meet a guy who would be so honest... Ed, you bastard... Come back...

EDWARD **walks out.**

Scene 22

EDWARD has been summoned to HEKTOR's office.

HEKTOR   You've defected to the enemy.

EDWARD   I went to offer my condolences. It's not a sin to offer condolence, is it?

HEKTOR   Are you a preacher?

EDWARD   No, sir!

HEKTOR   You act like one.

EDWARD   I have a right to share my grief with someone.

KENDRA walks in.

KENDRA   Being a movie star is not exactly sharing your grief.

HEKTOR   *(to EDWARD)* Do you think I wouldn't have known what you did?

EDWARD   Why did you call me here?

KENDRA pushes a stack of printed emails at him.

KENDRA   Did you write these emails?

EDWARD   I don't want to stay here for one more minute.

KENDRA   Answer my question, Ed!

EDWARD   Yes, I wrote those emails.

HEKTOR   You stole pages from my file.

EDWARD looks at KENDRA.

Don't look at her. Look at yourself. You stole, you spied, and you broke the law! Why?

EDWARD   Because I can't take it anymore!

KENDRA   You asked the boys to stop fighting.

EDWARD   I asked them to fight for freedom.

HEKTOR   Ed, we've freed countries more screwed up than Iraq.

EDWARD	But you can't free Ahad's daughter's body.
HEKTOR	He might stab you in the back, Ed.
EDWARD	Commander, do you know why we're scared of Ahad? Not because he's threatened to avenge his child's death, but because the deaths of thousands of children have become a mirror in which we see ourselves. You think we're scared of a terrorist? We're terrified of ourselves and what we've done.
HEKTOR	Are you a patriot or a traitor?
EDWARD	I'm a patriot, sir.
HEKTOR	Therefore, I have a plan for you. You'll go on the radio and say you're a patriot. You'll tell the boys that you're sorry to have sat next to Ahad. Tell the mothers and fathers back home that you haven't betrayed them.
EDWARD	I won't lie.
HEKTOR	Cut the crap, Ed.
EDWARD	I won't lie about a child we murdered.
HEKTOR	Murdered?
EDWARD	You prevented Ahad from giving blood. I could have saved her life.
KENDRA	Let me tell you something, Ed: You need to save your life. Sit down.

She pushes him into a chair.

	The army will drop the court martial if it has a retraction from you.
EDWARD	Saying what?
HEKTOR	You made a mistake by taping the film with Ahad.
EDWARD	I don't think so.
HEKTOR	You don't think, the army thinks for you: The army, God, and the country.

EDWARD starts to leave.

HEKTOR You don't have my permission to leave.

EDWARD I don't want your permission.

EDWARD **walks out.** KENDRA **and** HEKTOR **stand, stunned.**

Scene 23

KENDRA and HEKTOR in HEKTOR's office a short while later..

KENDRA | Why isn't anyone signing contracts?

HEKTOR | Ahad keeps reminding them that we are killing kids. And one of our men, Ed that is, your boyfriend, has partnered with Ahad. How do you expect anyone to have confidence in us?

His cellphone rings. He answers.

Yes, speak of the devil... we were just talking about him.

His eyes widen.

(loudly) What?... Goddamn... Who did that?

KENDRA | What happened?

HEKTOR | Somebody attacked Ed.

KENDRA | What—

HEKTOR | He's hurt... fatally—

KENDRA | Oh my God... Oh my God... where is he—

HEKTOR | Calm down... Kendra—

KENDRA | Who did it?

They rush out.

Scene 24

Captain EDWARD's coffin is wrapped in an American flag. KENDRA and HEKTOR stand over it. SAMIR is in the room with them.

HEKTOR
I'm truly sorry, Kendra. Last night I dreamt I was in the final moments of my life. Alone in a country I didn't recognize. I was dying, Ed was alive, and he came and sat with me.

SAMIR comes close to them.

SAMIR
I share your grief. I was just getting to know him better and—

KENDRA
Thank you!

SAMIR
He was a good man.

KENDRA
I told him to get out—

SAMIR
He wasn't the kind of man who would quit—

KENDRA
Thank you for your sympathies.

SAMIR
They are rejoicing.

KENDRA clearly doesn't know who SAMIR is speaking of.

Sheik gave a speech. He said fatwa has been fulfilled. He mentioned Omar and Ed's name and the crowd roared.

KENDRA
But Omar and Ed had become friends.

SAMIR
Who cares? The streets are full of men. They are shaking hands and touching their chests.

KENDRA
What does that mean?

SAMIR
It means insanity has gripped them. They don't know who the captain was but they're rejoicing his death.

KENDRA starts to leave.

KENDRA
Ed was a man of conscience.

SAMIR **walks up to** HEKTOR.

HEKTOR	His murder is a big blow for me, personally.
SAMIR	For me too.
HEKTOR	Why to you?
SAMIR	We were starting to have some important conversations. I was supposed to meet him that night; he was to tell me something important. He had some valuable information that the UN would have liked to know.
HEKTOR	I'll rearrest him.
SAMIR	Omar?
HEKTOR	Yup!
SAMIR	Why?
HEKTOR	I don't like jerks that first befriend then betray.

EDWARD**'s body is carried out with full military honour.**

Scene 25

> OMAR has been rearrested. He sits in an interrogation chair under a shaft of light. HEKTOR throws a newspaper at him with a gruesome photograph of EDWARD on it.

OMAR	I didn't kill Captain Edward.
HEKTOR	Then who?
OMAR	Men you pay to kill.
HEKTOR	I pay to kill?
OMAR	People are killing for survival.
HEKTOR	What kind of people are they?
OMAR	They are good for you, Commander, because they kill for cheap. Your war budget is drying up so you must find cheaper ways to kill. You've created the killing industry—
HEKTOR	Shut up.
OMAR	Now Iraqis are killing Iraqis.
HEKTOR	Ed wasn't an Iraqi.
OMAR	That is why it was stupid to kill him. Utterly stupid because the captain was a good man!
HEKTOR	You met him personally, didn't you?
OMAR	He said he was deeply sorry when he came to see me.
HEKTOR	Did you accept his apology?
OMAR	How could you accept your daughter's death simply because someone said "I am sorry"?
HEKTOR	He was really sorry.
OMAR	He truly was. He was aghast that you prevented him from helping my wife!
HEKTOR	What did you tell him about me?
OMAR	Everything!

HEKTOR	Goddamn!
OMAR	He asked if Congress knows what you've done.
HEKTOR	Go on!
OMAR	I showed him this.

He pulls out a photo.

Do you remember this man? Do you, Commander?

HEKTOR is silent. OMAR pulls out few other photographs.

Do you recognize yourself with these men?

HEKTOR	You showed him these?

OMAR brings out a document.

OMAR	And this. Read the date, Commander! I supplied you with the names of men who had grown comfortable with killing and executions and stealing—the fiercest one was the Butcher... you kept him in power.
HEKTOR	I had no part in this.
OMAR	Commander, you initialled every page. I took the risk of being an informer because I trusted you.
HEKTOR	You betrayed your people.
OMAR	You betrayed me.
HEKTOR	"The poet warrior, bending his gaze from his own heart, betrays himself." Your poem, Omar?
OMAR	I exposed the Butcher's treachery and you let him throw me in jail.
HEKTOR	Why would I do that?
OMAR	Because I knew too much about him and too much about you. I knew everything you did with him. Things that you didn't want anyone to know—
HEKTOR	I have nothing to hide.
OMAR	Oh you do, Commander. Do you know what they did to

me? I was tortured for speaking out. My brother was tied up. His pregnant wife was raped in front of him. My brother's skull was cracked open with a hammer; his wife's stomach was cut open and the baby scooped out and put in her mouth. Do you remember your handshake with the Butcher?

HEKTOR   That was before he lost his mind.

OMAR   He didn't lose his mind—just his luck, like other dictators who outlive their usefulness to America. When you got him, you kept me in jail to keep me silenced.

HEKTOR   You're not silenced.

OMAR   Your lies grew bigger by the day. You fed on power and forgot about me... Now I am going to make sure the truth comes out. It's not possible to silence me.

HEKTOR   It is.

OMAR   Are you going to torture me?

HEKTOR   Too easy.

OMAR   Kill me?

HEKTOR   Too little.

OMAR   Then what?

HEKTOR   Your daughter's body mutilated beyond recognition.

OMAR   You wouldn't dare.

HEKTOR   Your wife's body flung from a speeding car—hijab over her face, throat cut, and tongue dangling through the slit.

OMAR   Son of a bitch.

HEKTOR   Or I can set you free right now.

OMAR   What?

HEKTOR   Force you into exile. You enjoy too much attention in Iraq.

OMAR   If I refuse?

HEKTOR	You arrogant son of a bitch, can't you see death is looking you straight in the eyes? Ahmed...
OMAR	I won't go into exile. Never! You can't make me.
HEKTOR	Watch me.
OMAR	You watch me! The entire world is watching me. Everyone wants to know what you'd do to me after killing my daughter. I'm not going to give you the luxury to expel me so you have it easy here.
HEKTOR	You refuse?
OMAR	I refuse!
HEKTOR	Watch me, then. Ahmed...

AHMED **takes** OMAR. **The sounds of prisoners being beaten, dogs barking, and a hose.** HEKTOR **paces back and forth in a pensive mood. He goes to the telephone.**

Kendra, I want to see you...

Scene 26

HEKTOR's office.

HEKTOR	So that's how it is, Kendra. The man refuses to budge. A top US soldier, one who has won wars all over the world, now depends on the whim of a betrayer who won't accept exile.
KENDRA	And the world is beginning to question you. What is your connection to Ahad?
HEKTOR	Have you ever seen a man like me? Have you? Look at my medals—Vietnam, Philippines, Panama, Nicaragua, Rhodesia. Thirteen trophies to my name. And here I am; I've got to deal with an obstinate man—

KENDRA attempts to cut in.

	No, don't stop me, I know what you're going to say, I can read your mind, but no, let me tell you most resolutely, I've done no wrong.
KENDRA	Ed told me—
HEKTOR	Ed was one of my finest men.
KENDRA	What about this undercover meeting with Omar?
HEKTOR	I did have an undercover meeting with him.
KENDRA	So Omar is right.
HEKTOR	This happens in my business all the time—
KENDRA	Signing deals underground?
HEKTOR	That did not happen. Just because I met with him undercover doesn't mean I put my signature on something. He is blackmailing me.
KENDRA	Why did Ed not believe you?
HEKTOR	Because Ed took a liking to Omar Ahad. He felt for the dead girl, and for her mother.
KENDRA	Ed said—

HEKTOR	Whatever Ed said must be the truth. I'm sure Ed would only speak the truth. But whatever Ahad said to Ed isn't the truth.
KENDRA	What do you think Ahad told Ed?
HEKTOR	He probably said, "You could have saved my daughter."
KENDRA	He probably could have...
HEKTOR	No one knows...
KENDRA	But—
HEKTOR	But the truth is the truth—and the truth is that for the unfortunate death of one girl, we have saved millions of children from dying—
KENDRA	Yes.
HEKTOR	That is why we don't have to be blackmailed. In my business, in your business, there's so much that is undercover, so much that happens behind the scenes, and there are always two parties. What would you say when one party distorts and blackmails the other party?
KENDRA	Why didn't you tell me this before?
HEKTOR	I'm telling you now.
KENDRA	And why didn't you tell this to the world in those words, why didn't you say this to the UN and to the conference?
HEKTOR	To protect my family!
KENDRA	You never talked about your family before.
HEKTOR	Because I want to keep them out of this! Kendra, I was going to retire after this war. I didn't want to admit any blemish that will make them lose respect for me. Wouldn't you if you were me?
KENDRA	I don't have a family.
HEKTOR	Well I have. My old woman, my sons, my daughters, and my grandchildren. They are already being killed every day by reading it all in the newspapers. If I admitted that I met Ahad undercover—they would believe the rest of

the allegations. Kendra, I've made my share of mistakes. Maybe I should have stood up to the blackmail, but now I am squeezed. It is not only me but the conference and the reputation of our country—

KENDRA   The country has been pretty good to us—gives us money to screw things up and gives us money to fix the screw-ups.

HEKTOR   And money changing hands—

KENDRA   That too—

HEKTOR   Ending up in the prime minister's pocket for his flunkies who overeat and get drunk.

KENDRA   Or ending up in army generals' Swiss accounts.

HEKTOR   Or simply in closets.

KENDRA is taken aback. HEKTOR continues, ignoring her reaction.

Nobody is completely clean. So we have to choose. This man, this terrorist—for reasons of US national security I met him undercover and how does he pay me back? He distorts the truth! Who is he? He uses his daughter as a political shield and prevents his wife from leaving. He tapes an interview with Ed and then assassinates him.

KENDRA   I am personally hurt by that.

HEKTOR   So I ask you, can we let this man bully us? Blackmail us? Doesn't he worry you after what he did to Ed?

KENDRA   We don't know who did that...

HEKTOR   But at least you know me and Ed. One hundred percent Americans, from good families, symbols of our country. But this guy has created friction between us, between me and Ed, and doing everything to derail the conference. Can you afford that?

KENDRA   I will talk to his wife and to Samir and convince this guy to accept exile.

HEKTOR   And let him take with him all the secrets, all the evidence, the film, or anything he has on me. Let him take his daughter's body that has given him the limelight he wouldn't have had. I cannot be more generous—let him.

KENDRA

You don't fear he will talk?

HEKTOR

It will be his word against mine—but for now I want him out of the spotlight so he doesn't spoil our victory and your conference.

KENDRA

I will talk to Samir. I will talk to his wife—woman to woman.

HEKTOR

She is sensible.

KENDRA

We both have suffered losses. We'll understand each other.

KENDRA **exits.** HEKTOR **watches her go and then takes a deep breath.**

Scene 27

KENDRA, NAHLA, **and** SAMIR **visit** OMAR **in his jail cell.**

KENDRA **and** SAMIR **stay back a certain distance.** NAHLA **talks to** OMAR **alone.**

NAHLA	Omar, accept it.
OMAR	Why?
NAHLA	Here you go again.
OMAR	The attention of the world is on me.
NAHLA	It's your delusion.
OMAR	There *you* go again.
NAHLA	Do you really think you're liberating your country? Do you really think this jail is the headquarters of your liberation? Wake up, Omar.

OMAR **stares at her.**

Oh don't look at me like that.

OMAR	I want to be in my country.
NAHLA	Your country is not your wife. If you want to live with me, come with me; if you don't, you'll die here.
OMAR	At least I will die honourably.
NAHLA	Now coming with me has become dishonourable to you? I'm sick of your lunacy.
OMAR	Why did you stay with me for so long then?
NAHLA	Do I need to explain to you why I stayed with you? Why I was crazed for you, followed you here from Canada where I had a great life, friends, and family? I stayed back here after Ghazal's death even though I had an opportunity to leave. Now you ask me why?

KENDRA **walks up to him.** SAMIR **follows.**

KENDRA	Mrs. Ahad—let me try talking to Mr. Ahad.

NAHLA	Good luck.
KENDRA	Mr. Ahad, there's something either you don't understand or don't want to understand. Do you love this jail?
OMAR	I love this country.
NAHLA	Here he goes again.
OMAR	And my friends...
KENDRA	Well, I'll let them go with you.
OMAR	You will?

KENDRA looks at SAMIR.

SAMIR	Except you won't find them.
OMAR	Why?
SAMIR	Most have already accepted exile.
NAHLA	*(to OMAR)* Would you now leave? Not for your daughter but for your friends who've already fled?
SAMIR	Omar, let me tell you something that you should already know. Hektor will hand you over to the prime minister and he will torture you to death as an example for those who might see you as an inspiration. You'll be locked away, blinded, deafened, and given to prison rats that have gotten used to human flesh. Would you prefer that?
OMAR	How can I do my work from exile?
KENDRA	If you go into exile now you can tell the world your story. If you don't you'll die in jail.

SAMIR gives the film to KENDRA.

OMAR	Is Hektor not worried?
SAMIR	You should be worried.
KENDRA	Hektor just wants you out of his sight because you've become a headache for him.
OMAR	You're confusing me.

KENDRA	Look at your wife and imagine what your life could be...
OMAR	I'm in a fix here.
KENDRA	...and what you can accomplish in exile.
OMAR	Accomplish? Can I get my daughter?
NAHLA	At least we can give her a proper funeral. And if you don't, Omar, I am going because the commander is releasing the body.
OMAR	Wait...

He starts walking to NAHLA. KENDRA offers him the exile document and a pen to sign with.

KENDRA	Take my pen and put your signature on this. Say goodbye to this jail. Fifty of your trusted men are waiting to leave with you. Your plane will be leaving in thirty minutes.

We hear AHMED directing traffic.

Scene 28

A military transport plane is idling on a runway. AHMED is escorting people onto the plane.

AHMED

You, sir, quick, climb on! You're clear. Climb on. And you... can't carry that, what do you think—you're going shopping?

At the airfield.

SAMIR

There is your luggage. Everything you wanted to take, in that suitcase. You have your documents, your film with Ed, your interview with me. Everything!

Ghazal's coffin is taken to the plane.

OMAR

What is that?

SAMIR

That is Ghazal.

NAHLA steps closer to OMAR.

AHMED

Ten minutes. Omar Abdul Ahad, climb aboard.

OMAR boards the plane. KENDRA starts to leave.

OMAR

Thank you, Ms. Kendra.

SAMIR gives OMAR a hug.

AHMED

Hey, UN guy... Why aren't you going?

SAMIR

I'll stay here for you.

SAMIR and KENDRA watch as the plane takes off.

We hear OMAR and NAHLA on the plane.

OMAR *(offstage)*

I love you.

NAHLA *(offstage)*

I love you too.

OMAR *(offstage)*

To Montreal!

NAHLA *(offstage)*

To the house we lived in.

OMAR *(offstage)*

It won't be easy without Ghazal.

HEKTOR's office. He is in a meeting with the PRIME MINISTER.

PRIME MINISTER
Commander, I have been reading the conditions and terms of the agreements Madame Kendra has proposed...

HEKTOR
And?

PRIME MINISTER
The document entitled "Foreign Suitors for Iraqi Oil Fields and Raw Materials"?

HEKTOR
What about it?

PRIME MINISTER
I don't see many Iraqi names in it.

HEKTOR
You have to read carefully. There is a strategy in it and it is not really a sinister strategy.

The plane explodes. HEKTOR seems unaffected by the sound. KENDRA charges into his office.

KENDRA
Hektor!

HEKTOR
I was just telling the prime minister—all is well.

KENDRA
What just happened?

HEKTOR
Would you do me a favour?

KENDRA
What just happened?

HEKTOR
Would you go to the closet and see what's in there?

KENDRA walks out of HEKTOR's office. She sees AHMED standing nearby in an open field.

AHMED
I'm sorry, an Arab doesn't kill a brother. The captain was like a brother. They made me do that. I am not guilty— the bullet in your head was marked with the supplier's name.

KENDRA stands alone, holding the tape SAMIR had made.

EDWARD (offstage)
I cannot accept that among the dead there are no innocents, and I cannot accept that I couldn't help your daughter... I am sorry... That is why I wanted to come and

tell you all personally... I am sorry...

GHAZAL *(offstage)*   Baba, come home.

NAHLA *(offstage)*   Ghazal, look what Baba wrote for you.

GHAZAL *(offstage)*   I don't want his poetry.

OMAR *(offstage)*   You don't?

GHAZAL *(offstage)*   I need you. Baba, come home. Come home, Baba... Come home.

The end.

What the press and the public say about Truth and Treason

Despite the saturation by the news media of the tragic stories from Iraq, the message conveyed by your writing was fresh, intense and captivating. The simplicity of the sets and the high caliber of the acting did justice to your fine work.

It has been a long time since I had the opportunity to watch live theatre, but the performance on Friday has rekindled my interest in this art form. Congratulations!

– Jaspal S. Rangi, www.monsooncorporatebusinessgifts.com

Truth and Treason is an important play that should be seen widely. The quality of the extensive research and thinking invested in this work is awesome in the truest sense. Congratulations on being able to carve some focus and clarity out of such complexity. As a result, the audience is able to appreciate the enormity of the situation in Iraq without being overwhelmed by it. Only then can anything resembling thoughtfulness be brought to bear in the search for the truth (should it exist).

The play was beautifully staged, yet in a way that allowed us to concentrate on the text and its delivery by the actors, all of whom did very fine work.

– Shelley Tepperman, dramaturge, and Vadney Haynes, playwright

There is an old saying that the first casualty of war is truth; this has to be extended to include the distortion and misinterpretation of truth to justify launching wars.

One walks away from the play thinking about the futility of war to "solve" human rights abuses, be it the subjugation of minorities or women. Wars create many more problems than they solve. The solution is much worse than the problem, akin to amputating an arm to take care of a painful boil on a finger.

We had read the review of the play in The Gazette and went to see the play with a degree of trepidation. We think that the critic had not got it right. The play presents a sweeping and effective denunciation of the war and lives up to the Teesri Duniya motto "change the world, one play at a time."

– Sushma and Biren Prasada, Kabir Cultural Centre

I thought the play was terrific with all the complexity and ambiguity of the situation fully wrung out. The staging and sound were also very impressive.

– Peter White, Art Curator

Congratulations!! My friend Qais and I were deeply moved by your excellent play – a well written, fluidly directed and designed anti-war production. The panel was enriching with profound comments on the role of arts in time of war.

I liked your definition of the aim of a playwright when he or she is writing the piece as an art form. It is about honest characterization and aesthetics as key elements to communicate art successfully to the audience. Another subtle aspect is that of relationships. Overall the play comes across as a very insightful depiction of the machinery of war and its sub-theme that eventually "war/power corrupts all of us" (that is understatement).

Thank you very much for bringing the reality of War to all of us. Tanvir Sahib would have been rightly proud of this superb production. Am sure it will inspire viewers to look at the truth as it is.

– Balwant Bhaneja, Playwright and translator

My greatest congratulations to you and your team for your show. It is clearly and undoubtedly, your best work ever. The script was very well written, acting was excellent, the set was outstanding, direction was strong and the whole piece worked seamlessly together! Fantastic! I was too moved to talk for a good while after the play. Bravo! Thank you!

– Janet Lumb, artistic director, Asian Heritage Festival

On the behalf of my dad and I, I wanted to extend my/our warmest congratulations on your magnificient play. I think, Rahul this is your finest work yet! It was powerful, tight in its presentation and execution and the pacing was spot on. (The lighting, sound and production/set design was brilliant). In particular, it was a stellar production in its casting choices; it seemed like I was watching movie. I was struck by the imagery in the play- beautiful, haunting. It would translate quite well into film. I suppose I would have to commend the play's director – it seemed like she was a perfect fit. Bravo!

– Eisha Marjara, Film maker

The set for *Truth and Treason* is a mostly empty stage hung with a patchwork of curtains. Behind certain of the curtains in the patchwork are small, tight spaces where the victims or critics of the United States Commander's machinations are shown trying to figure out how to thwart him. When they succeed at coming up with a way to do so, they die. Beautiful choreography elevates their deaths to tragedy and points up one more crucial truth: the victimizers are also victims of their own treachery. They also fall.

– Jane Gilchrist, Actress and playwright